I Lost My Nose

Richard Hernandez
Illustrated by Lisa Brenman

Copyright © 2023 **R.Hernandez Publishing**

All rights reserved. No part of this publication may be reproduced, distributed, or transmitted in any form or by any means, including photocopying, recording, or other electronic or mechanical methods, without the prior written permission of the publisher, except in the case of brief quotations embodied in critical reviews and certain other noncommercial uses permitted by copyright law. For permission requests, write to the publisher, addressed "Attention: Book Rights and Permission," at the address below.

Published in the United States of America

ISBN 978-1-962110-87-7 (SC)
ISBN 978-1-962110-85-3 (HC)
ISBN 978-1-962110-86-0 (Ebook)

R.Hernandez Publishing
222 West 6th Street
Suite 400, San Pedro, CA, 90731
leerentals@hotmail.com

Order Information and Rights Permission:

Quantity sales. Special discounts might be available on quantity purchases by corporations, associations, and others. For details, contact the publisher at the address above.

For Book Rights Adaptation and other Rights Permission. Call us at toll-free 1-888-945-8513 or send us an email at admin@stellarliterary.com.

Dedication

To my dear wife. My fiercest critic, my biggest fan. And for all the years she's stood by my side.

I'd be remiss if I didn't mention my grown children, Richard and Deeana who have graced us by being all we could have wished. And let's not forget the little monster granddaughters. The love of our lives.

Book Description

I lost My Nose is a fascinating trip into a young boy's imagination. Day after day his flights of fantasy lead him into fabulous daydreams. Join him and enjoy the ride.

Book Summary

I Lost My Nose, a pleasing romp through a young boys' vivid imagination. Daydreaming as only a young person can.

Author's Biography

As a young man, I too had a vivid imagination. Books transported me. Science fiction and science fantasy were my first loves. By the fourth grade, writing had become my second passion. Reading and writing have stayed with me my entire life. Remember: Always feed the child in you. Laugh and never be afraid to dream.

This morning I sat up in bed

I felt so out of place

Hopped out of bed to start my day
I went to wash my face

Can you imagine how I felt
The shock, oh no, the fear!
When in the mirror I did see
It's gone, oh my, my ear!

I ran real quick back to my room

And looked upon the bed

And there it was, right where it fell

My ear fell off my head

Back to the mirror I did go

To glue the ear back on

And almost fainted when I saw

My nose, it too, was gone!

I raced around and I did shout

My nose I could not find

Then dizziness, I felt, oh no!

Could I be going blind?

The room was spinning quickly now

To the mirror I did run

Oh what a shock, was I surprised

To see not two, but one!

One wide-eyed eye was all I had

How could this weird thing be?

And if I lose the other eye

Blind as a bat I'd be

Went rushing 'round, with just one eye

Not much there was to see

Without an ear, a nose an eye

What would become of me?

I searched the room, beneath the bed

With one eye I did seek

Thank goodness that I had my mouth

Or soon I could not speak

Not finding anything, I tried

To stand but fell back down

That's when I saw my leg was gone

How could I get around?

I hopped and hopped, went round and round

Went crashing into walls

With just one eye and just one leg

I could not help but fall

My room I should have cleaned real well

Like I was told to do

How could I've known I'd trip and fall

On books and my old shoes?

At last I fell onto my bed

As tired as could be

I closed my eye, gave one deep sigh

No hope was left for me

The next thing that my ears did hear
A sound that was so sweet
Was mother calling out to me
Get up, get on your feet!

It's late, to school you need to go

Please hurry up and dress

And when you get back home from school

You need to clean this mess

I touched my face and found
Two eyes
Two ears, and yes, my nose!
With joy I jumped right out
Of bed
I had two legs, ten toes.

A dream was all, that I
Did have
I had not lost my nose
So off to school I'd quickly go
If I could find my clothes